MAGIC QUESTIONS

A Children's Book that Encourages Curious Questions

WRITTEN BY
RUBY CRUZ

Copyright © 2022 Ruby Cruz
Cruzruby18@gmail.com

ISBN 979-8-218-48546-7

Library of Congress Control Number: 2024916159

Published in Inglewood, California, United States of America
First Printing, 2024

Special thanks to my momma, Ella Cruz.

I wrote this book for all of the children around the world.

I want you to know that there is nothing you can't do.

The magic ingredient to being all you can be is to use your voice to ask all the questions you want to ask.

Without asking questions, you will never know the answer.

By asking questions,
you help yourself and the world.

Remember,

you are smart, brave, and funny.

You are one of a kind.

Do you want to know why
you should be curious?

You should ask all the questions
you want because . . .

There is only one you,
and you matter.

You are a
smart person.

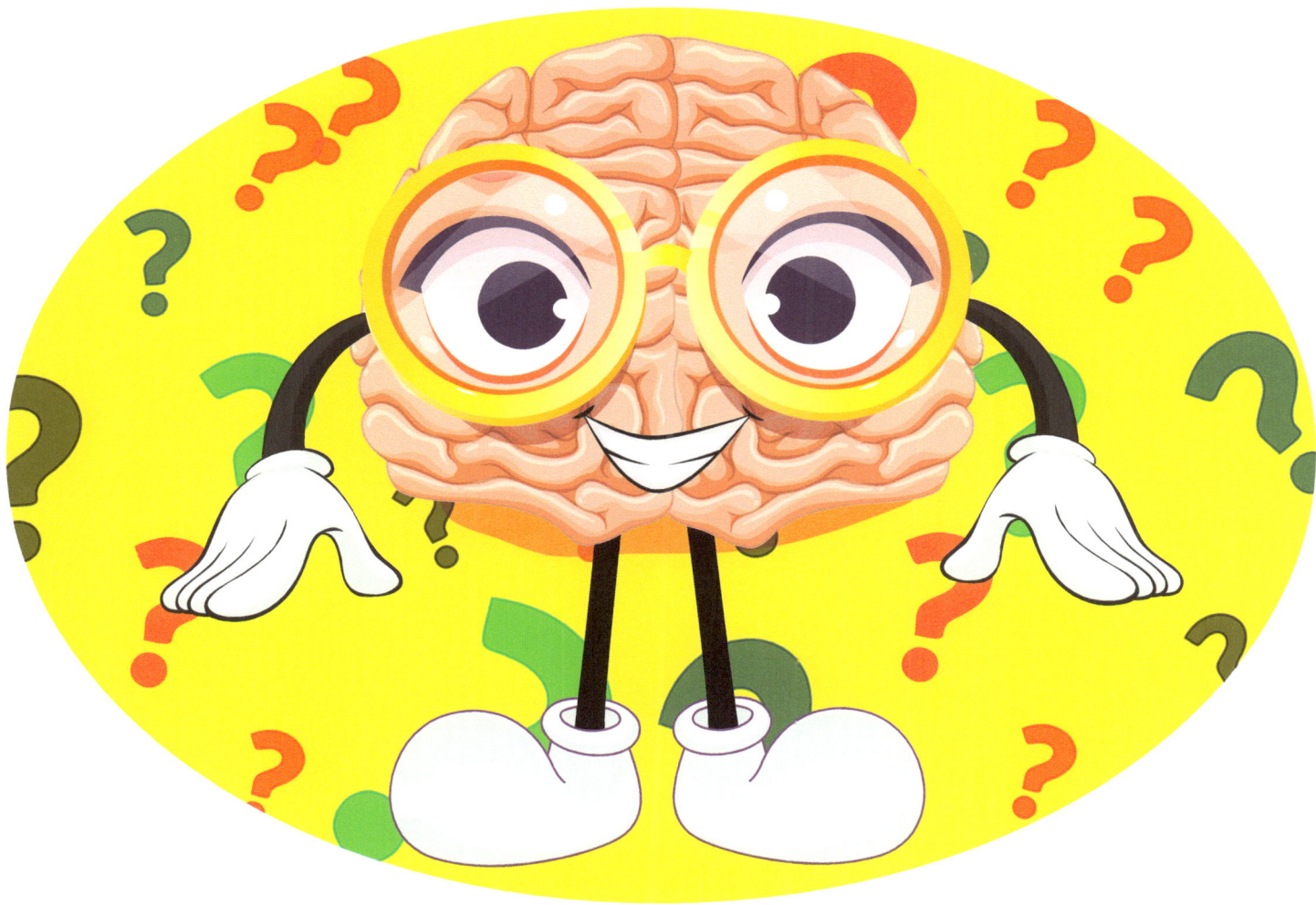

You are a
funny person.

When you ask questions,
you change the world.

Asking a lot of questions
shows imagination.

Asking a lot of questions
takes courage.

Asking a lot of questions
makes you smart.

Asking a lot of questions helps us all understand things, so don't stop!

How does one
become a
hero?

By asking
questions.

How does one
know how
to do things?

By asking
questions.

How does one
person help
another person?

By asking
questions.

Do you want
to know what
makes you *you?*

It is simple.
Ask
questions.

The questions you ask
shape who you are.

You see the world better, and others see a new way too.

Your questions
make you *you!*

Never be afraid
to ask questions.

Questions are
your magic and superpower.
Shine bright!

Hi, I'm Ruby Cruz.

I'm a young adult but will always be a kid at heart.
Listed below are some fun facts about me. Please enjoy!

- I love to laugh
- Yellow is my favorite color
- I love peanut butter sandwiches
- Sunflowers bring me joy
- I am brave
- I am strong
- I am smart
- I enjoy asking questions
- Dancing makes me happy
- I love the beach
- I like cartoons
- I enjoy exercising
- I love snails

It makes me happy
to know that you are
reading this book.
I hope your day is filled
with lots of surprises,
good food, and laughter.

www.ingramcontent.com/pod-product-compliance
Lightning Source LLC
Chambersburg PA
CBHW060825270326
41931CB00002B/62